How To

LIVE FOREVER

LIVE FOREVER

By NICK ARNOLD

Illustrated by
Tim Benton

FRANKLIN WATTS
A Division of Scholastic Inc.
New York Toronto London Auckland Sydney
Mexico City New Delhi Hong Kong
Danbury, Connecticut

First published 2001 by Oxford University Press
Great Clarendon Street, Oxford OX2 6DP

First American edition 2001 by Franklin Watts
A Division of Scholastic Inc.
90 Sherman Turnpike
Danbury, CT 06816

Catalog details are available from the Library of Congress
Cataloging-in-Publication Data

ISBN 0-531-14641-3 (lib. bdg.) 0-531-14818-1 (pbk.)

Printed in China

Contents

HOW TO LIVE FOREVER

In Kyoto, Japan, there is a beautiful temple garden in which three fountains gush and splash. According to legend, each fountain has magical powers: "Drink from the first fountain and you'll become rich. Drink from the second fountain and you'll find love. Drink from the third fountain and you'll enjoy a long and happy life."

Which fountain would you choose?

Wouldn't most of us choose a long and happy life? For thousands of years people have dreamed of fountains of youth and elixirs of life, magical things that could make them live forever. This dream is coming closer to reality every day! People are living longer than ever before, and some scientists are talking excitedly about extending human life for hundreds of years. Find out how as you read about

☞ killer diseases and how to beat them

☞ why your dog can expect to live longer than your hamster

☞ how to avoid stress and stay healthy

☞ the foods that can help you live longer

☞ how worms can teach us to live forever

☞ how to replace your old body parts with new ones

CHAPTER ONE

MEDICAL MARVELS

People who think they know about science will tell you that all living things grow old and die. They claim that aging and death are laws of nature. But there are some living things that seem to go on forever.

In the heart of California's Mojave Desert is a dusty creosote bush. It's not much to look at, but this humble shrub, known as "King Clone," is over twelve thousand years old. Just think—it was alive before there were wheels or pyramids! It's even older than California's bristlecone pine trees, which are mere saplings at five thousand years old.

Young upstart!

If you take a peek through a microscope at a drop of pond water, you might be able to spot another amazing elderly organism—a tiny creature called a hydra. It multiplies by growing babies on its body like buds, but the adult hydra shows no sign of old age. And that's not all—certain roundworms cut in half will live as long as a worm that hatched from an egg. That means if a roundworm were cut in half every few weeks, it really could go on living forever!

So here's the $64,000 question:

Well, humans are already living far longer than they used to. This is because of marvelous medical discoveries that help people survive diseases that would have finished them off in the past. Read on for a full medical report.

Medicine Gets Its Act Together ....

The practice of medicine started in China around 400 B.C., when the emperor decreed that only people with special medical training could be doctors. Meanwhile, the ancient Greek Hippocrates (460–370 B.C.) laid the foundations of medicine in Europe by training doctors to look for the signs of disease in order to spot what the illness was. This is called diagnosis.

The Greeks didn't get everything right. They thought illness was caused by an imbalance of four vital fluids in the body—blood, phlegm, yellow bile, and black bile. For two thousand years, doctors believed this nonsense and cheerfully slapped squirming, slimy leeches on critically ill people to suck their blood. The patients were thought to have too much blood, and this grisly treatment was supposed to make them better. It never worked. Today, however, leeches are successfully used in some types of surgery to keep the blood flowing.

For two thousand years, doctors treated sick people without understanding the actual causes of disease. All this time, killer diseases such as the plague (a disease spread by rats and fleas, sometimes known in history as the Black Death) and smallpox claimed thousands of victims. Then, in the 1790s, the first clues fell into place—thanks to a cow, a milkmaid, and a heroic little boy.

The First Vaccination?

Country doctor Edward Jenner (1749–1823) was a real bore. He would chatter on to fellow doctors about his belief that catching a skin ailment called cowpox would prevent the far more deadly disease of smallpox. It was twenty years before he tested his idea in a dramatic fashion. First he took pus from the hand of Sara Nelmes, a young milkmaid suffering from cowpox, and scratched it into the skin of James Phipps, the child of one of his patients.

➤

Can you imagine your doctor using you for medical experiments?

Think that was bad? The next part is much worse.

James suffered from the mild skin sores of cowpox. A few months later, he was injected with pus from a smallpox sufferer. But wait... wasn't smallpox deadly?

Smallpox was the worst disease in the world. If you want to know what it was like, imagine a face covered in sores that itched and rotted and scarred the flesh. The disease killed one-third of its victims. Would James suffer this terrible death? The anxious weeks passed, but despite a slight fever, the boy remained healthy. Dr. Jenner had proved his point, and soon everyone wanted cowpox treatment. This was an early form of vaccination.

What Is Vaccination? . . . .

Every time you get sick, your immune system swings into action to destroy the germs that are making you sick. An army of tiny living units called white blood cells identifies the attackers and makes proteins called antibodies that stick the germs together. Then more white blood cells gobble the germs up. Vaccination means giving the body weakened or dead germs so that the white cells can get to know them. Then they will recognize and fight the living bugs if they ever get inside your body. Although no one knew it at the time, the cowpox germ was similar enough to the smallpox germ to fool the white blood cells into thinking they were the same.

I'd know you anywhere!

In Edward Jenner's time, doctors still didn't know about germs or how they caused disease. This crucial discovery was made by French scientist Louis Pasteur (1822–1895).

Mr. Bacteria:
Louis Pasteur

Pasteur lived for his work. He worked so hard and was so interested in microscopes that he even used one to examine his food at mealtimes. In 1862, he showed that germs were tiny living things (we now call them bacteria) that live in the air and cause disease.

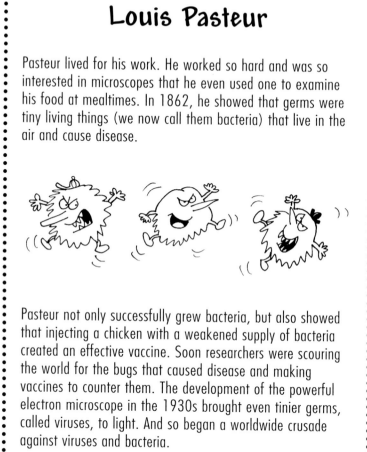

Pasteur not only successfully grew bacteria, but also showed that injecting a chicken with a weakened supply of bacteria created an effective vaccine. Soon researchers were scouring the world for the bugs that caused disease and making vaccines to counter them. The development of the powerful electron microscope in the 1930s brought even tinier germs, called viruses, to light. And so began a worldwide crusade against viruses and bacteria.

By 1980, humans had gained their greatest-ever victory over disease. An international campaign wiped smallpox from the face of the Earth. Edward Jenner would have been mighty proud.

The Deadly Cut

An understanding of germs wasn't just good news for sufferers of disease; it made surgery a lot safer, too. Let's take a quick trip back in time to 1830.

This patient is having his injured leg cut off. The surgeon is rather proud of his unwashed apron encrusted with dried blood—it proves he's experienced.

The patient is screaming because pain-killing gases haven't been invented yet (they were first used in 1842). At least the surgeon is quick—the best of them can whip off a leg in 30 seconds. Unfortunately, the patient's survival chances are only 50/50—yikes!

The problem here isn't pain or loss of blood. The problem is that the operating room is crawling with germs that happily make their home in the patient's wounds. The stump of the leg rots, and the patient dies.

Germ-Killer: Joseph Lister

Enter a rather unpunctual but very hardworking surgeon, Joseph Lister (1827–1912).

Inspired by Louis Pasteur's work, Lister tries drenching his operating room in germ-killers. His favorite is carbolic acid, a substance used to disinfect sewers. In 1865, a young boy named James Greenlees is brought to Lister. The boy's leg has been crushed by a cart, and it seems there is only one thing to do—chop it off and hope the boy lives. But Lister has other ideas.

He washes the boy's leg in carbolic acid and wraps it in foil, allowing the broken bones to set. Normally the leg would start to rot as bacteria get to work, but the acid kills the germs. In six weeks, Greenlees has recovered! It's a medical marvel, and Lister's fellow surgeons slowly come around to the idea of using germ-killers. Over the years, keeping operating rooms germ-free saves thousands of lives.

In the nineteenth century, life was unhealthy and short. Poor people often had to drink water that was full of sewage. Diseases such as cholera, which are caused by drinking germ-laden water, flourished. In 1854, cholera killed hundreds of people in London. Fearless medical researcher John Snow (1813–1858) tracked the disease down to a particular water pump that stood a few feet from a leaking toilet. People were drinking water swarming with cholera germs from the terrible toilet!

This was before Pasteur had made his discoveries about germs, so Snow didn't understand that cholera germs caused disease. But his work inspired doctors and politicians to campaign for clean water supplies and better housing. As living conditions improved, people became healthier and began to live longer.

Even more lives were to be saved and lengthened thanks to a lazy doctor who became famous because he went on vacation.

Fun with Fungus: Alexander Fleming

In 1928, a sloppy germ researcher left his London lab and set off on his summer vacation. Alexander Fleming (1881–1955) was too lazy to dispose of his dishes of growing germs, and he got a shock on his return. On one dish, the germs had been attacked and killed by a mystery fungus. Actually, Fleming didn't notice this, but someone pointed it out before the scientist washed the dish. As a result of this discovery, millions of lives were to be saved.

At that time, Fleming realized the fungus wasn't powerful enough to kill germs in humans, and nothing happened for a few years. Then, in 1940, policeman and amateur gardener Albert Alexander scratched himself on his roses. The scratch was deadly.

Germs from the thorns attacked Alexander's face and bones, and soon he was gravely ill.

Science to the Rescue?.........................

Then scientists from Oxford University, led by a dynamic Australian named Howard Florey, started dosing Alexander with a new drug called penicillin. It was made from the purified juice of a fungus similar to that discovered by Fleming. For a few weeks the treatment seemed to work, and Alexander recovered. But the juice began to run low, so they had to start recycling it from Alexander's urine. In spite of their efforts, the juice ran out and the policeman died. The lesson was clear—penicillin could save lives, but only if there was enough to go around.

Florey's colleague, Norman Heatley, helped an American firm mass-produce the drug, and by the end of World War II (1939–1945), penicillin was being used to treat injured soldiers. Millions of people were saved from disease and infected wounds. But more was to follow. Penicillin was the first of many new drugs called antibiotics, developed from natural germ-killing substances. In 1952, Selman Waksman (1888–1973) made an antibiotic called streptomycin from a fungus that he found in the throat of a sick chicken. The new antibiotics proved their worth against killer diseases such as tuberculosis and the plague.

By the 1960s, it looked like infectious disease was going to be a thing of the past.

CHAPTER TWO

MEDICAL MIRACLES

Aren't we lucky to live at a time when medicine has begun to put an end to disease? Now all we have to do is figure out how to live forever!

Um... no.

Thanks to the benefits of modern medicine, better housing, cleaner water, and more food, people are living longer than ever before. In the 1880s, one in four children died before they were old enough to go to school. In any ten years of their lives, they had a one-in-ten chance of kicking the bucket. Most people didn't make it to age forty-six, and fewer than one in four made it to sixty-five. There wasn't anything very good about the "good old days."

By the 1990s, most people in the developed world were living past age seventy-six. In 2000, one British family celebrated the arrival of a special baby.

21

For the first time ever, there were six generations alive at the same time. Besides the mom, there was a granny, a great granny, a great great granny, and a great great great granny!

But people still die of disease. Not so much from the plague or cholera, although these diseases are still killing people in poorer parts of the world, where antibiotics are in short supply. Instead, people are suffering from other diseases, such as cancer and heart disease. And meanwhile, some of the old favorites have been staging a comeback.

This chapter is about how doctors have been tackling these threats and dreaming up some amazing new technologies to help.

Cruel Cancer ....

There's actually nothing new about cancer. Some
Egyptians suffered from the disease.

But because cancer tends to develop later in life,
in the past most people died before they could
develop the illness. Now people live longer, and the
disease is more common. Today cancer causes 13
percent of deaths worldwide, and the disease accounts
for 1 in 4 deaths in wealthy countries.

Cells in Crisis

The human body is made up of millions of tiny units called
cells. Most cells are so small that 50 placed in a line would
measure only about .04 inch (1 millimeter). It's possible that
your body contains 100 trillion cells. Don't even think about
checking this—it would take you over 3 million years to count
them all!

➤

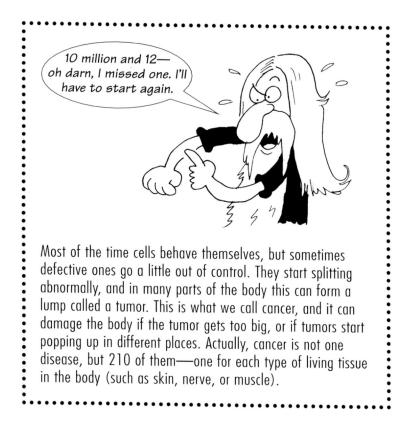

Most of the time cells behave themselves, but sometimes defective ones go a little out of control. They start splitting abnormally, and in many parts of the body this can form a lump called a tumor. This is what we call cancer, and it can damage the body if the tumor gets too big, or if tumors start popping up in different places. Actually, cancer is not one disease, but 210 of them—one for each type of living tissue in the body (such as skin, nerve, or muscle).

Cancer treatment can involve removing a tumor by surgery, poisoning it with chemicals (chemotherapy), or zapping it with radioactive rays (radiotherapy). The problem with chemotherapy and radiation is that they can kill off healthy cells, too. But at last help is at hand. For decades scientists have been searching for a cure for cancer, and time is running out for these dreaded illnesses. Doctors are developing and testing new treatments that will hopefully be cancer killers in the future. Let's meet the magnificent four: gene therapy, gamma knife, polymer bullets, and blood vessel inhibitors.

Gene Therapy.....................................

Gene therapy means targeting deoxyribonucleic acid (DNA), the complex chemical that controls cell functions. (To find out about DNA and genes, turn to page 47.) Cancer is caused by faulty DNA that makes cells divide all the time. Gene therapy tries to fix this problem by introducing the correct DNA to the affected cells.

Gamma Knife ....

This treatment sounds like something from a science-fiction film, but it's actually quite simple. Instead of blasting the affected area with radiation, doctors target their firepower on the tumor. A gamma knife zaps a brain tumor with 201 beams of high-energy radiation from all directions. It's accurate enough to avoid damaging the healthy parts of the brain.

Polymer Bullets...............................

Instead of putting poison in the entire body, scientists are developing tiny capsules that deliver a steady dose of poison to a cancerous tumor. The capsules are made of a substance called a polymer, designed to dissolve slowly inside the body and release the poison over a set period.

Blood Vessel Inhibitors.......................

Just like any other part of the body, a tumor needs a supply of blood to survive. The blood brings oxygen and sugars for the cells to feed on, and without it the tumor will shrink or die. Scientists have found natural chemicals called inhibitors that prevent blood vessels from forming around a tumor and thus stop it from growing. These chemicals could also be used to shrink the tumor.

Spies in the Body ....

Before doctors can attack a tumor, they need to know exactly where it is. These days it's getting easier to spot tumors wherever they're lurking. Endoscopes are viewing tubes that can be inserted into any opening in the body with little damage. There is also magnetic resonance imaging (MRI), a technique that uses a combination of powerful magnets and radio waves to produce a computer-generated picture of what's going on inside the body. It images the radio waves that bounce back from each area to produce a moving picture of what's going on in all of your parts.

Horrible Heart Disease . . . .

In many parts of Europe and North America, heart disease is a bigger killer than cancer. The heart is an amazing example of natural engineering. It's basically a pump that works nonstop for an entire lifetime, squirting blood around the body and to the lungs to receive oxygen from the air. It beats four billion times in an average lifetime, and each beat is powerful enough to send a red blood cell from your heart to the end of your leg and back again in just 12 seconds. But the heart can go wrong.

Broken Hearts and Battered Brains . . . .

Fatty chemicals can build up in the vessels that supply the heart with blood. These chemicals can place strain on the heart so that it wears out more quickly. The arteries that take blood to the major parts of the body can wear out, and the buildup of damage causes blood clots. These stop the blood from flowing to the heart and can cause a heart attack, when the heart stops beating properly.

Blood clots or tearing of the brain's blood vessels can stop oxygen from getting through, so parts of the brain die. This is called a stroke.

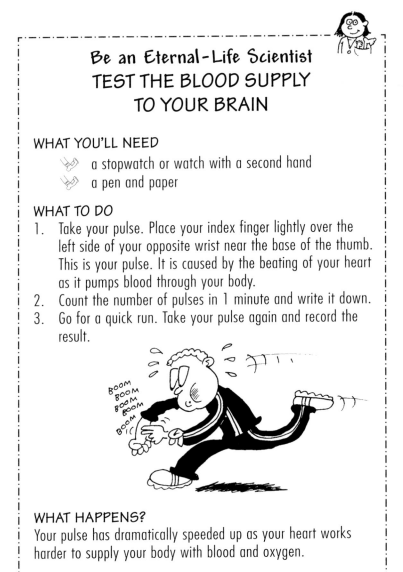

Be an Eternal-Life Scientist
TEST THE BLOOD SUPPLY TO YOUR BRAIN

WHAT YOU'LL NEED
- a stopwatch or watch with a second hand
- a pen and paper

WHAT TO DO
1. Take your pulse. Place your index finger lightly over the left side of your opposite wrist near the base of the thumb. This is your pulse. It is caused by the beating of your heart as it pumps blood through your body.
2. Count the number of pulses in 1 minute and write it down.
3. Go for a quick run. Take your pulse again and record the result.

WHAT HAPPENS?
Your pulse has dramatically speeded up as your heart works harder to supply your body with blood and oxygen.

Transplant Technology ....

One way to deal with a failed heart or any other body part is to replace it with a transplant. The first successful transplants were kidney transplants in 1954. Today the list of body parts that can be transplanted is growing longer. Heart transplants and liver transplants are now pretty common. And transplants might have a big role in the future. In 1998, surgeons in Lyon, France, gave a New Zealander an arm cut from a dead man. And in 2000, they sewed two new arms onto a Frenchman who had lost the use of his own arms in a fireworks accident.

But let's look further ahead, to the hospitals of the future.

Be sick at St. Future's Hospital! All diseases treated!

Relax on a robot bed that automatically measures your heart rate and blood pressure.

Hospital pajamas with intelligent sensors monitor your blood sugar, heartbeat, and body temperature.

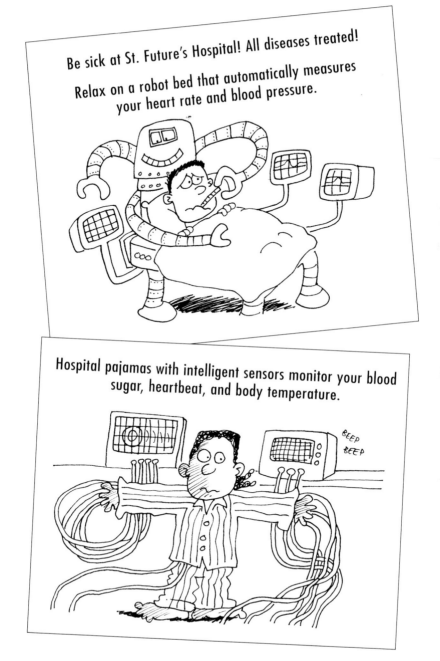

Beds supply automatic emergency oxygen, heart massage, and electric shocks to restart your heart if it fails!

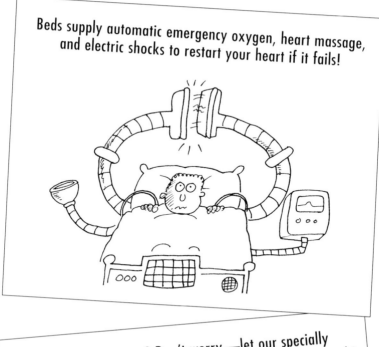

Need an operation? Don't worry—let our specially programmed nanorobots (each the size of a cell) do the job! Relax on your robot bed while the tiny surgeons go to work inside your body!

Medical Note: These robot beds and sensitive pajamas can be made using the inexpensive silicon-chip microsensors that scientists are predicting will be available by 2030. Nanomachines already exist, and tiny robot surgeons may be a reality by 2040.

Did Anyone Mention Diseases? . . . .

Just when you thought it was safe to sit on the bus next to someone who keeps blowing his nose, along comes a new army of diseases—as well as some old favorites.

The new diseases appearing on the scene are viruses that have lived for thousands of years in wild creatures such as apes, mice, and blood-sucking insects. The diseases haven't done us any harm because we didn't have much contact with the animals that spread them. But thanks to our habit of destroying forests, we are coming into contact with more and more new viruses, and as people travel more by air, these diseases can spread quickly around the world.

The worst disease so far is autoimmune deficiency syndrome (AIDS), which destroys part of the immune system. Without this protection from germs, the body eventually becomes very ill and dies. AIDS can only be contracted from infected blood or body fluids (not from toilet seats or toothbrushes). Even so, nineteen million people have already died from the disease.

To make matters worse, some nasties from the past have come back to haunt us. The lung disease tuberculosis (TB) and the mosquito-carried disease malaria were thought to be under control. But then new strains of TB and malaria started to appear, and drugs couldn't kill them. The diseases were drug-resistant. Every year malaria infects 500 million victims, mainly in tropical parts of the world, and TB is now one of the world's biggest killers.

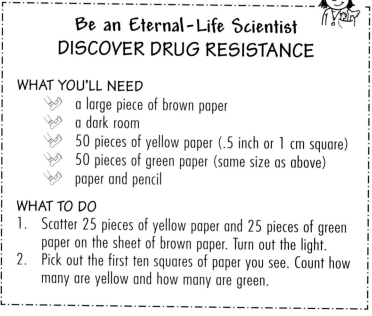

Be an Eternal-Life Scientist
DISCOVER DRUG RESISTANCE

WHAT YOU'LL NEED
- a large piece of brown paper
- a dark room
- 50 pieces of yellow paper (.5 inch or 1 cm square)
- 50 pieces of green paper (same size as above)
- paper and pencil

WHAT TO DO
1. Scatter 25 pieces of yellow paper and 25 pieces of green paper on the sheet of brown paper. Turn out the light.
2. Pick out the first ten squares of paper you see. Count how many are yellow and how many are green.

3. Bacteria increase their numbers by splitting in half. Switch the light on and add two pieces of yellow paper for each yellow piece remaining and two pieces of green paper for each green piece.

4. Repeat steps 2 and 3 twice more.

WHAT HAPPENS?

1. There should be fewer and fewer yellow squares because they are easier to spot in the weak light. The yellow squares are like bacteria that are vulnerable to antibiotics.

2. There should be more and more green squares. These squares increase like antibiotic-resistant bacteria. The bacteria can multiply faster because there is less competition from other bacteria for food and space.

But don't panic—doctors and scientists won't give up! Modern medicine is fighting back with an armory of new weapons.

New Improved Drugs ....

Antibiotics stop bacteria from dividing, and some kill bacteria by destroying the protective walls that surround them. Drug-resistant kinds of bacteria pump antibiotics back out of their bodies or make chemicals that switch off the antibiotics that try to attack them. Scientists are designing new antibiotics that disable the defenses of the bacteria.

Vaccines ....

The best way to protect the body from disease is by using vaccines. In the 1960s, measles affected 500,000 American children every year, causing fever, skin rash and, in some rare cases, death. But thanks to a vaccine introduced in 1963, measles has all but vanished from most countries. The polio vaccine has also been effective in driving a harmful disease from many countries. Health professionals are currently trying to wipe out polio in all parts of the world.

Since 1993, scientists have been developing a new breed of vaccines based on the DNA of viruses. Just one slice of this DNA is enough to prepare the immune system to fight off the virus.

So, despite the setbacks, we're still making progress. Medicine can still help us fight diseases that try to cut our lives short. But there's one condition we still can't cure: aging itself. If you really want to live forever, you'll have to do something to stop getting older. But what?

CHAPTER THREE

GETTING ON A BIT

Before you start reading this chapter, think about this. Do you *really* want to live forever? Here's a legend from ancient Greece that might make you think twice.

A Cautionary Tale

In ancient Greece, a man named Tithonus was going out with the goddess of the dawn, Eos. The goddess noticed that her mortal boyfriend was growing older. Of course, being a goddess, she never aged. So she asked her dad Zeus, the king of the gods, to make Tithonus live forever.

Anything for you, darling.

So Tithonus didn't die—but he kept on aging. His hair became white, and his teeth fell out. He became slow, wrinkly, deaf, and blind. Each day Tithonus would sing to himself in a voice that became squeaky and cracked with age. At last Eos could stand it no longer, and she asked good old Dad to get rid of him. Taking pity on his daughter, Zeus turned poor old Tithonus into a cicada insect! And, the story goes, Tithonus is still around today. You might come across him singing to himself in his raspy little voice and looking as ancient and dried-up as ever.

Got the message? It's no use living forever if you can't avoid the effects of aging. But what exactly are these effects? And what causes them? The next pages will show you what to look out for.

before   after

39

WARNING!
Before inspecting your grandparents for signs of
aging, you ought to know that not all older people
suffer from all of these effects, and they might be
quite upset if you tell them they do!

1. Wrinkles. Old people have plenty of these. As
    you get older, the skin loses cells and becomes
    less springy and elastic. As the skin fails to
    spring back into shape after folding, it gradually
    creases into wrinkles. (To make a wrinkle, try
    frowning 200,000 times.)

2. Sagging skin. As the skin becomes less elastic, it
    droops down under the influence of gravity. This
    is especially obvious under the eyes and chin
    (causing a double chin) and the ear lobes.

3. A man's hair thins out on top, while more
    hair sprouts from his nostrils and ears.
    Scientists aren't too sure why this
    happens. Hair turns gray because
    each hair loses color and
    becomes hollow
    inside, reflecting
    the light in a way
    that makes the
    hair appear
    gray or white.

    Switch off the light!

4. The heart, lungs, and muscles weaken. This is partly due to cells dying off and partly due to lack of exercise.

5. Older people often suffer from stiff, swollen joints. This painful condition is called arthritis.

6. The eyeballs and their lenses bulge slightly, making it hard for the eye to focus on close-up things. Older people often need glasses to correct their vision.

7. The senses of smell and taste weaken as cells die in the smell receptors of the nose and the tastebuds on the tongue. By the age of seventy, 50 percent of the sense of smell is gone.

8. Older people's hearing weakens as the bones inside their ears become stiff. Cells die off in the hearing mechanism of the inner ear.

9. Cells might die off in a region of the brain that controls the storage of memory. Although the memory remains as good as ever, an older person finds it harder to recall the information.

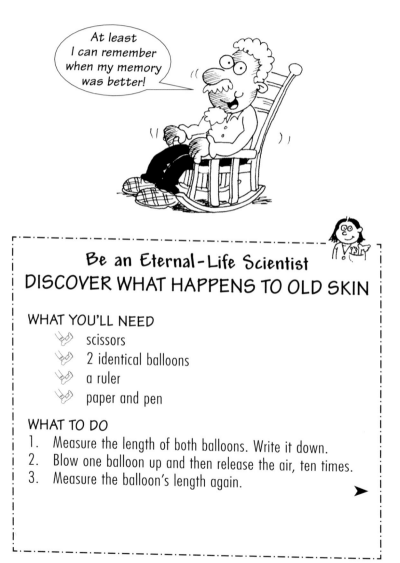

Be an Eternal-Life Scientist
DISCOVER WHAT HAPPENS TO OLD SKIN

WHAT YOU'LL NEED
- scissors
- 2 identical balloons
- a ruler
- paper and pen

WHAT TO DO
1. Measure the length of both balloons. Write it down.
2. Blow one balloon up and then release the air, ten times.
3. Measure the balloon's length again.

➤

WHAT HAPPENS?
The balloon that has been blown up is now longer. This is because after being stretched and used a lot, it has lost its elasticity. It starts to sag the way aging skin does.

Hey, Gramps!

Hormone Hopes ································

So that's what happens physically. Now for the tricky part—explaining why. You see, aging doesn't have a single cause; it has several. They include

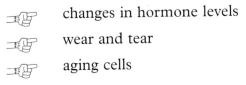 changes in hormone levels

wear and tear

aging cells

Okay, so what are hormones? Hormones are chemicals that float around in the blood and produce changes in the body. For example, hormones made by the thyroid gland in the neck control how fast the body's cells burn up sugar to make energy. Human growth hormone, made by the pituitary gland in the brain, makes the body grow.

As a person gets older, the amount of growth hormone in his or her body decreases. But what happens if the body is given extra hormones? In 1990, Daniel Rudman of the Medical College of Wisconsin gave Fred, a retired mechanic, injections of human growth hormone. The results were incredible. Fred began to look younger, and his muscles got bigger.

Unfortunately, Fred also developed aches and pains, and when the injections ceased, his muscles shrank again.

The Dangers of Everyday Life ....

Now for the second cause of aging. Don't panic, but every day your body is under attack! Day after day, the pressures of life are aging your body. To find out more, we're going to take a quick look at leaves.

Be an Eternal-Life Scientist
DISCOVER HOW LEAVES GET DAMAGED

This experiment works best in late summer or early autumn, when the leaves have been growing through the summer months.

WHAT YOU'LL NEED
- a selection of damaged leaves from different plants
- a magnifying glass

WHAT TO DO
Study the leaves. Use the magnifying glass to examine them more closely.

WHAT HAPPENS?
You may find several kinds of damage: holes made by various munching insects, slugs, and snails, or spots caused by disease or by the plant dumping waste chemicals in the leaf. In other words, plants suffer from wear and tear over time.

I need a vacation!

But What's This Got to Do with Humans?

Humans also suffer from wear and tear (although luckily our bodies can repair themselves, which is why our wounds heal). Here are a few of the rigors of everyday life our bodies face:

- Harmful chemicals, such as bleach, damage and dry the skin.

- Tobacco smoke is bad news for the body. It wrinkles the skin, clogs the lungs with tar, and causes lung diseases and cancer. Chemicals in the smoke enter the bloodstream and cause clogged blood vessels and a greater chance of heart disease.

- Teeth decay and fall out because of the kinds of food we eat and because we don't always clean our teeth properly.

- Heavy drinking of alcohol can damage the liver and make it harder for the body to process food or break down poisons.

- Wounds and some skin diseases can leave scars.

- Joints become overused and develop arthritis (see page 41).

- Ulcers can cause scarring on the inside of the stomach and intestines.

- Looking at the sun too long damages eyes.

- Sunlight contains ultraviolet rays that can damage the DNA in skin and make it look all dried up, or even cause skin cancer.

Aside from all this wear and tear, your cells are dying off, and this also causes aging. To understand this, you need to know a bit more about DNA.

DNA and Its Secrets

Scientists had long suspected that cells contained a chemical code that controlled how they developed. Then, in 1953, Francis Crick and James Watson figured out the structure of this chemical, DNA. DNA is like a ladder that has been twisted into a corkscrew shape by a circus strongman. The rungs of the ladder are a combination of four chemicals called base pairs. The code to make the cell grow and develop is the exact order of the base pairs in the ladder. Inside the cell, each unit of DNA is organized into a structure called a chromosome. Humans have forty-six chromosomes (twenty-three pairs). Got all that?

We did it!

Every feature of your body, such as your eye color, is coded by units of DNA known as genes and made up of thousands of base pairs. Human DNA contains over 100,000 genes, and in recent years scientists have finished mapping where each gene is located on the chromosomes. You may have heard of this vast undertaking, known as the Human Genome Project.

This is a big job. If you lined up the entire DNA in just one human cell, it would be almost 6.5 feet (2 meters) long. If you wrote the human DNA code down, it would fill a 500,000-page book, and if you attempted to translate the code into English, you would fill over a thousand huge encyclopedias!

Where's the part about blue eyes?

Smashed-Up Cells ....

Much of what we call "aging" is caused by cells in each part of the body gradually dying off. But why do cells die? Why don't they last forever so we can too?

A cell might be tiny, but it's incredibly complicated. Imagine a cell as a tiny factory. Like every factory, it uses power. Ripping apart tiny molecules of glucose supplied in the blood produces the cell's power. This creates energy, but it also creates harmful electrically charged chemicals called free radicals, which can damage DNA.

Although DNA has its own repair mechanisms, damage can build up and eventually prevent the DNA from controlling the cell. Sometimes the cell starts dividing and causes cancer. And worse still, any possible repair work seems to slow down as a person grows older.

Cures for Old Age ....

As you can imagine, people will try anything to reverse the signs of aging. Below are just a few of the crazy things people have tried in the past. (*Don't* try any of these at home!)

Blood Baths

In the 1600s, Hungarian Countess Elizabeth B'athory bathed in blood to stay young. She even tried drinking it, too. This mad woman even had a handy machine designed for stabbing and bleeding young girls. Unfortunately for Liz, bathing in blood doesn't keep you young—and it's against the law. The crazy countess was locked up for life after murdering more than six hundred girls.

Doggy Snacks

How about "eating" ground-up bits of dog or guinea pig? In 1889, Professor Charles Brown-Sequard tried it. He thought it would make him feel like a new person and live longer. Surprise, surprise! The loony prof puréed his pets for nothing! The body's immune system destroyed the injected material. Brown-Sequard ended up covered in sores from the injections and died at the not remarkably old age of 77.

Yogurt for Youth

Nobel Prize-winning scientist Elie Mechnikov (1845–1916) ate lots of yogurt. He believed the living yogurt bacteria would stop any harmful bacteria from moving in. Although yogurt is a very healthy food, there's no proof that it actually extends life.

So, is that it? Perhaps you're wondering if you have any chance at all of living forever, because aging affects us all, and these remedies aren't worth much. Well, wonder no more. There are things you can do to slow down the aging process. Read on and find out!

CHAPTER FOUR

FIT FOR LIFE?

This chapter is about how to live longer. First we're going to meet a person who ought to know the secret if anyone does: the oldest woman in the world.

Pampo's Story

One January day in 1875, a baby girl was born on the West Indian island of Dominica. She was christened Elizabeth, but she became known to everyone as Pampo. When she was a little girl, Pampo had no toys, and she never went to school or saw a doctor. Her mother was too poor to afford any of these luxuries. As soon as she could walk, Pampo worked from dawn to dusk in the sugarcane fields.

Sometimes Pampo's mom sent her to buy food from the nearest store, a whole day's walk away.

You'll have to go back. You forgot the butter!

Pampo never had any great adventures, and the most exciting event of her life was her wedding day, when she visited a local town. Sadly, she didn't have a happy life—her only son died in his forties, and she lost contact with her remaining family. But Pampo lived on.

At the dawn of the new millennium, Pampo was still living in her shack by the sea just as she had in the previous century—and the century before that. She had never gone away on vacation, had an electric light, or owned a phone or a car. She was 125 years old, yet somehow time had passed her by. What was her secret?

Pampo's Secret....................................

Pampo told a reporter that the reason she lived such a long time was her healthy diet. She ate lots of fresh fruit and vegetables and drank fresh coconut milk.

Although Pampo didn't know it, these foods are rich in chemicals called antioxidants. Cells that protect DNA from free radical damage use these. (Free radicals are the electrically charged chemicals that can damage DNA.)

Be an Eternal-Life Scientist
MAKE A LIFE-EXTENDING FRUIT SALAD

WHAT YOU'LL NEED
- some fresh dates (if you can't get these, the dried variety will do)
- a coconut
- a banana
- a mango

WHAT YOU DO
1. Ask an adult to drill a hole in the coconut and drain out the milk.
2. Peel and chop up the banana and ask an adult to chop the mango and the dates, removing the pits.
3. Ask an adult to saw the coconut in half and scoop out some of the flesh from the coconut.

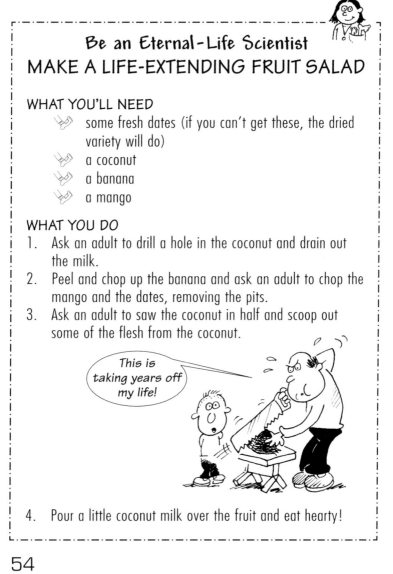

This is taking years off my life!

4. Pour a little coconut milk over the fruit and eat hearty!

And now for some more healthy tips for a long life.

Live Long, Live Healthy

1. Brush your teeth twice a day. Brushing lightly with circular movements using a soft nylon brush.
2. Get plenty of exercise. This doesn't mean running a marathon every day. It means biking or walking daily and not being too lazy to run errands.

3. Avoid eating too much candy and potato chips, especially just before a meal, when they could spoil your appetite.
4. Never stay out in the sun for more than a few minutes without using a strong sunblock. Wear long sleeves and long pants if you are in the sun for long periods of time.

There's another factor that affects how long you live—and you really can't do much about this next one.

Do Women Live Longer Than Men? ....

Not necessarily. Figures show that on average women die at an older age than men do, but that doesn't tell the whole story. The figures show that the important factor is that men die younger. Confused? Here's why.

Young men spend more time outside the home and are more likely to die in accidents or by violence. As they grow older, men are more likely to get certain cancers (it's thought that a hormone called estrogen helps protect women from some of these). However, if men don't smoke or drink alcohol and eat healthy food, they can still live as long as women. And speaking of food, here's a rather strange question.

Is Lack of Food Good for You? ....

In the 1930s, scientists made an amazing discovery. Mice kept on about one-third their normal intake of food lived one-third longer than normal.

I'd do anything for a lump of cheese!

Their diet included all the necessary vitamins, and oddly enough, these mice had as much energy as before. This finding has been repeated with other creatures, such as worms and apes. So could it be true for humans? Could a human live to be 150 just by missing a few dinners? And what's causing this effect?

Scientists think that lack of food switches DNA off. When this happens, the DNA is tightly wrapped in a layer of protective chemicals. This acts like bubble wrap, shielding the DNA from damage by those nasty free radicals.

Whatever the cause, some scientists are already cutting down on their food intake in an attempt to live longer.

WARNING!
Don't cut down on your food while you're growing up.
Your growing body needs all the grub it can get!

Healthy Body and Healthy Mind ....

If you're really serious about living forever, you'll need to look after your mind as well as your body. It's no use staying healthy and youthful if your brain turns to jelly! It helps to learn new things whenever possible (why not read some more books in this series?), practice your problem-solving skills with puzzles or computer games, and enjoy lots of hobbies. You'll also need to learn how to deal with a horrible monster called stress.

Sickening Stress

Stress is how you feel when you're all keyed up—pulse racing, muscles tense, palms sweating. Stress can be quite a useful bodily reaction. Just imagine—it's the Stone Age, and you've got to fight a cave bear.

A little stress might come in handy here. The fast pulse is a sign of oxygen-rich blood zooming around your body to those tensed, action-ready muscles. The sweat flowing helps keep those heat-producing muscles from overheating your body.

Stress is great for preparing your body for action. But when you feel stressed because you've got to do something like a test, it just makes you feel bad. And too much stress can even make you ill. Sickening, eh?

Study after study has shown that stress causes poor health. In the 1970s, scientist Hans Sleye found that stressed lab animals were more likely to get sick. In 1991, an experiment using humans seemed to confirm this. A group of college students were exposed to colds—some of the students were feeling stressed and some weren't. Nearly half the stressed students caught colds, but only a little over a quarter of the relaxed students ended up with red noses.

This finding is not to be sneezed at—it seems that stress switches off the immune system, leaving the body more vulnerable to germs.

If you want to stay healthy, it helps to relax and enjoy life. So pour yourself a nice cold drink, put your feet up, and read on. It's time for another glimpse into the future—this time it's a visit to Dr. Well's Health Clinic.

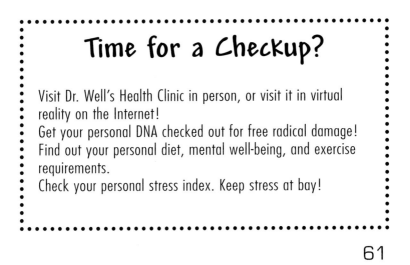

Time for a Checkup?

Visit Dr. Well's Health Clinic in person, or visit it in virtual reality on the Internet!
Get your personal DNA checked out for free radical damage!
Find out your personal diet, mental well-being, and exercise requirements.
Check your personal stress index. Keep stress at bay!

This isn't as far-fetched as it may sound. Doctors are beginning to realize that being relaxed and happy is an important part of keeping patients healthy.

The DNA check should be possible once human DNA has been completely decoded and understood, within about thirty years.

You say you don't like healthy food and exercise, and cutting down on food sounds like too much of a hardship? Okay, there's another way to live longer—if parts of your body are failing you, why not simply buy some new parts? Yes, it really is possible!

CHAPTER FIVE

TIME FOR A NEW BODY?

So, you want a new body?

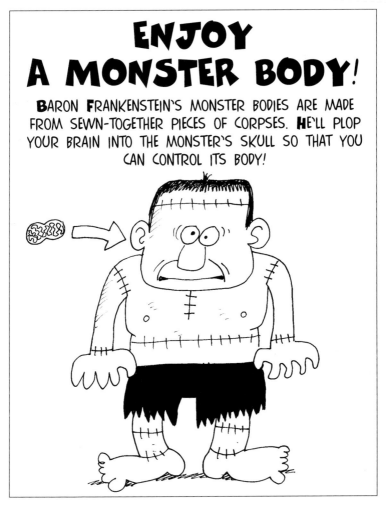

ENJOY A MONSTER BODY!

BARON FRANKENSTEIN'S MONSTER BODIES ARE MADE FROM SEWN-TOGETHER PIECES OF CORPSES. HE'LL PLOP YOUR BRAIN INTO THE MONSTER'S SKULL SO THAT YOU CAN CONTROL ITS BODY!

Don't panic! We won't really be trying that particular treatment. There are actually three options for getting a new body and living longer:

1. Rely on transplants as and when they are needed to replace your worn-out body parts.

2. Get some artificial body parts made and use them to replace the faulty living parts.

3. Grow replacement body parts from your own cells.

Transplant Troubles ....

There are two problems with transplants. First, the body's immune system attacks any tissue that it doesn't recognize. This is called rejection. Baron

We don't want this new heart!

Frankenstein's monster would have died quickly, because each part of the body would have rejected the other parts. That's why transplant patients need powerful drugs that switch off their immune systems for a while to stop this from happening.

Second, there is a shortage of spare organs that can be transplanted from dead people. (We're not talking musical instruments here, by the way—an organ is a body part with a particular job.) Scientists are trying to get around the shortage by breeding pigs with human DNA. When the pig organs are transplanted into humans, their human DNA should give them more chance of being accepted by the recipient's immune system.

Bionic Body Parts...............................

The other option is artificial body parts. In 1998, a Scottish hotel manager was given a bionic arm.

The arm was controlled by nerve signals from the remains of his old arm and a complex series of pulleys and gears. The arm could twist and grip and bend. It was even covered in a layer of silicone that looked like real skin. As time goes by, scientists are inventing more and more artificial body parts.

Body Parts

Here's a selection of artificial body parts. Some are still at the experimental stage but should be widely available in the next few years.

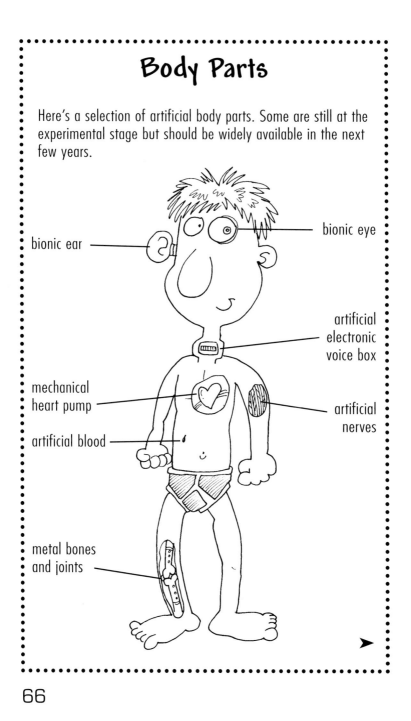

bionic ear

bionic eye

artificial electronic voice box

mechanical heart pump

artificial nerves

artificial blood

metal bones and joints

➤

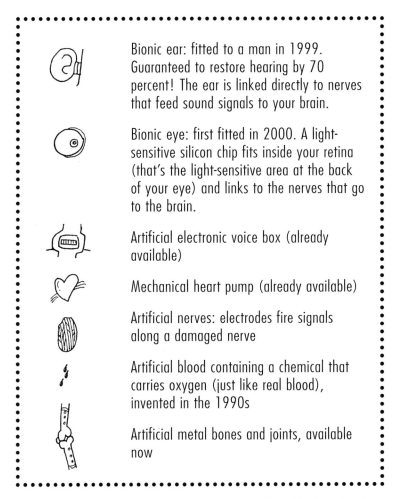

Bionic ear: fitted to a man in 1999. Guaranteed to restore hearing by 70 percent! The ear is linked directly to nerves that feed sound signals to your brain.

Bionic eye: first fitted in 2000. A light-sensitive silicon chip fits inside your retina (that's the light-sensitive area at the back of your eye) and links to the nerves that go to the brain.

Artificial electronic voice box (already available)

Mechanical heart pump (already available)

Artificial nerves: electrodes fire signals along a damaged nerve

Artificial blood containing a chemical that carries oxygen (just like real blood), invented in the 1990s

Artificial metal bones and joints, available now

One of the hardest parts to make artificially is a brain. After all, your brain stores your memories and personality. If you had an artificial computer brain, all this information would have to be downloaded from your real brain. Even so, some scientists are talking about being able to produce artificial brains by 2050! So you really could live forever—as long as you don't mind being a bionic robot!

Grow Your Own Body Parts ....

But there's another possibility. You could actually grow your own cells to make spare body parts for transplant.

Because they contain your very own DNA code, your immune system will think the new organs are part of you and won't attack them. Sound interesting? Okay, here's how to do it.

First, you're going to need to know about stem cells. These are the cells you'll be growing your organs from. The amazing thing about stem cells is that they don't age and die like other cells.

Stem Cell Secrets ....

You have stem cells in the lining of your mouth and intestines and in the marrow of your bones. Their job is to divide constantly and make new cells. Without them, your mouth and intestines would be worn away by your food and saliva.

Your stem cells are almost as old as you are. Every human starts off as an egg fertilized by a sperm cell.

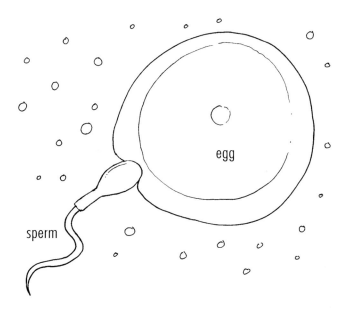

egg

sperm

The egg and sperm each contains half the DNA needed to build an entire human being. The sperm's DNA fuses with the egg's, and the egg begins to divide. In a few days it becomes a ball of cells, and each cell has the ability to divide and form new organs. These are your stem cells.

Make Your Own Body Parts
(Note: don't actually try this)

Take some of your DNA from a cell in your skin and stick it in an empty egg—a hen's egg will do. By the way, when we say "empty hen's egg," we don't mean an empty hen's eggshell—we mean the tiny cell inside the shell that could have developed into a chick. This cell is empty because its DNA has been removed.

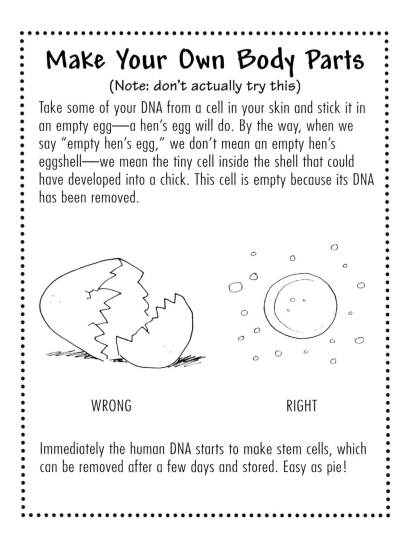

WRONG   RIGHT

Immediately the human DNA starts to make stem cells, which can be removed after a few days and stored. Easy as pie!

The fact that stem cells continue dividing for a long time could prove very useful. One day it might be possible to inject stem cells directly into any area of the body that needs regenerating. The stem cells would be programmed to work in just that area, and you wouldn't need messy, painful transplant surgery!

But for the moment this isn't possible. Unfortunately, scientists aren't too sure how the stem cells know which body part to form. In 1998, scientists at the University of Wisconsin grew cells for different body parts from stem cells simply by changing the food the cells were being fed. But DNA and chemical signals among the stem cells may also be important.

Scientists think that by providing a scaffolding of polymer for the cells to grow on, they can encourage the cells to form a new hand or a new heart, blood vessels, skin, or whatever you wish. They have already managed to grow a human ear inside the skin of a living mouse.

Amazing Alternatives ....

There is an amazing alternative to growing your own stem cells. Cancer cells also divide without aging, and one type of cancer has the ability to form body tissues such as teeth and hair in the wrong parts of the body. Scientists are planning to use these cancer cells to regrow worn-out body parts. And that's not all.

Scientists at the University of Philadelphia have found that when mice have their immune system switched off, they can regenerate their own bodies. Mice with damaged ears and tails can grow new ears and tails. They can even replace some of their nerves and bone and muscles. Although the scientists are not really sure why this happens, it's not unique. Salamanders and newts also regrow parts of their bodies, and certain lizards can lose their tails and regrow them.

If you could do this, you wouldn't age. Whenever a body part wore out, you could simply grow a new one. The only problem is that without an immune system, germs would attack you. The only way to survive would be to live in a germ-proof bubble.

So you wouldn't like spending eternity in a plastic prison? Well, there is a substance that keeps your cells alive forever, and guess what? It's inside your body at this very minute! Find out more in the next chapter.

CHAPTER SIX

MEAN GENES

Aging affects different people in different ways. Some people look ancient at forty, while others look young and glamorous in their seventies. This is why guessing someone's age can get you into trouble!

Looking youthful and living long seem to run in families. So there must be something people are born with that keeps them alive and looking young. There is, and that something is DNA. After all, you inherited half your forty-six chromosomes from your mom and half from your dad.

How Does DNA Affect Aging? ....

Every piece of DNA has its own fuse that turns the DNA into a ticking time bomb. The fuse is called a telomere, a protective cap that fits over the ends of each chromosome.

Be an Eternal-Life Scientist
FIND OUT HOW
A TELOMERE WORKS

WHAT YOU'LL NEED
- a length of string
- a piece of tape
- a piece of steel wool or any rough brush

WHAT TO DO
1. Wrap a piece of tape around one end of the string.
2. Brush the other end of the string roughly with the steel wool, then bang it on the end of a table ten times. Now brush and hit it again.
3. Repeat step 2 with the end of the string that is protected by sticky tape.

WHAT HAPPENS?
The unprotected end of the string becomes worn and frayed, but the protected end should remain undamaged. The tape works like a telomere protecting the end of a chromosome.

I'm afrayed I've had enough!

Each time a cell divides, the DNA replicates too, and some of the protective telomere is worn away. The longer the telomere, the longer the cell can survive. When the telomere is all gone, the DNA is left unprotected and can easily be damaged.

Cells That Live Forever..........................

So how come stem cells don't wear out? Well, it's because of a substance called telomerase. Telomerase rebuilds the telomeres. Stem cells (and cancer cells) make telomerase to rebuild their telomeres. That's why they don't age like ordinary cells. And the making of telomerase is controlled (surprise, surprise) by the DNA. So you know what that means, don't you? In your own body, you have the power to make cells that live forever!

A cell that makes this amazing stuff can never die. Scientists have even found the gene that orders a cell to make telomerase and added it to the cells of an old man. The cells started dividing, and even after four hundred divisions they were still going strong. The old man's cells had gained eternal youth!

But don't jump for joy just yet! If your body had this treatment it would last forever, but there are a few nitty-gritty problems to overcome first. Namely, how do you get the telomerase gene into every cell in your body? And how do you switch the gene on and off so that the cells don't divide all the time?

Meanwhile, scientists are searching for other genes that might have an effect on aging and how long we live. Their inspiration for these experiments comes from other animals.

Ancient Animals ....

Some animals live for a very long time. Flounder, lobsters, and sharks grow bigger as they get older, but they show no signs of aging. The only reason they ever die is because of disease or injury. Tortoises not only move slowly, but also age slowly. The oldest known giant tortoises lived over 175 years.

The oldest large animal is the elephant. Elephants live for up to eighty years. The oldest birds are parrots and eagles. They both live over forty years.

Be an Eternal-Life Scientist
FIGURE OUT THE AGES OF YOUR PETS

WHAT YOU'LL NEED

an old cat or dog (a friend, someone at school, or a neighbor might have one if you don't)

WHAT TO DO

Write down the age of the animal, and then figure out its equivalent in human years. A cat year is the equivalent of five human years. A dog year is the equivalent of six or seven human years.

Now answer the following questions.

1. Does the animal walk awkwardly, or is it stiff-legged? This might be a sign of arthritis.
2. Is the animal thin or overweight? Elderly cats tend to eat less and look thinner as their muscles waste away. Elderly dogs usually eat as much as ever and put on weight because they exercise less.
3. Does the animal show signs of hearing loss?

Older cats and dogs show signs of deafness. Also, the animal might not react to sounds as quickly as a youngster might.

➤

4. Does the animal urinate in the house?
   Aging shrinks the kidneys and makes the bladder less able to hold urine. Aging might also affect the animal's memory so that it forgets the training it received when it was young.

WHAT HAPPENS?

In some ways cats and dogs age like humans. They lose their hearing and develop problems that humans suffer in old age, such as heart disease and arthritis. But cats and dogs age faster than we do. Few cats live more than twenty years, and most dogs die between eight and fifteen years old.

So why does my dog live longer than my hamster?

Scientists aren't sure, but there's a theory that answers this question and explains the whole reason why animals age. It all has to do with natural selection.

Select for Survival

Over millions of years, every species (type) of plant and animal changes form in a process called evolution. For example, sixty million years ago, the first horses were just 12 inches (30 centimeters) tall! Evolution is powered by something called natural selection. Here's how natural selection might have worked with penguins.

At one time all penguins were black. Seals swimming underwater could easily spot their dark tummies and dart up to catch and eat them. Some penguins had white tummies, so the seals couldn't see them as easily. The penguins with white tummies had genes that made their tummies white. More of them survived to pass the genes on to their young, and over time all penguins were born with white tummies.

Now here's the crucial part. An animal can have really terrible aging genes and still pass the natural selection test! Even if an animal grows old quickly and dies young, as long as it lives long enough to produce offspring, it will pass on its genes. This helps explain why your dog ought to live longer than your hamster.

Hamsters can produce young when they are just ten weeks old. And once a hamster has had a few babies, there is no reason why its aging genes shouldn't kick in. So within sixteen months, most hamsters have gone to that great big hamster wheel in the sky.

But a dog can be a year old before it gives birth, and it might take another three months before the puppies can leave their mom. So dogs need to live longer to be sure of passing on their genes. It takes years for humans to have families and bring up their children, which is why we live far longer than either our dogs or our hamsters!

Learning from Animals ....

Scientists have found that we share surprisingly large amounts of our genes with our fellow animals. We share a whopping 40 percent of our genes with a roundworm and 75 percent with a mouse.

Already scientists have found genes that help extend the life of one type of worm. They have also found that one of these genes seems to be similar to a human gene that keeps cells alive.

So here's the big picture: your genes and DNA are pretty important. And if they're not up to scratch, the best that science can offer is the chance to get the right genes, or maybe a squirt of telomerase to protect your DNA. But if you're really set on living forever and don't mind being cold, there is yet another possibility to consider. How about a deep freeze?

CHAPTER SEVEN

COLD COMFORT

Just one look at the ancient bag of peas in your freezer should convince you that very cold temperatures preserve things. But can extreme cold really help people live longer?

Animals as different as bears and bumblebees go into a state of suspended animation known as hibernation in cold weather. In this state their bodies and heartbeats slow down, and their cells use up food far more slowly.

Could hibernation help slow the effects of aging? Humans don't hibernate, of course. But there have been cases of people who have fallen into freezing water and survived without air for up to ten minutes because the cold dramatically slowed the rate at which their cells needed oxygen.

A Real Cool Character

It's true that a frozen human can be preserved for a very long time. One cold night over five thousand years ago, a traveler went to sleep in a little hollow high in the Alps, the mountains that separate Austria and Italy. He never woke up. In 1991, walkers found his frozen body preserved in ice and surrounded by his clothes, tools, and weapons. Ötzi, as the body became known, had achieved a kind of immortality—despite not being alive.

Some people believe it might be possible to freeze their dead bodies and thaw them out at a later date to restore them to life. To do this, the bodies are drained of blood and filled with glycerol antifreeze. Next they are submerged in liquid nitrogen at a bitterly cold temperature (-320°F, or -196°C). This technique is known as cryogenic suspension.

But before you start filling in the application forms, you should know that things can go wrong.

Cold Comfort?....................................

The biggest problem with cryogenics is that no one knows how to bring a frozen body back to life. And while being preserved in liquid nitrogen, any water left in the body would have turned to ice, splintering and destroying the cells. The dead bodies would be too damaged to bring back to life, anyway.

There might be hope for the future, however. In the 1990s, scientists found out how to preserve organs for transplants. The organs were soaked in a liquid containing sugar and dried with a chemical called perfluorocarbon and stored at low temperatures.

Some Antarctic fish can survive temperatures of below freezing because their bodies contain natural antifreeze chemicals. So will we one day be able to preserve an entire human body? And could that person be revived?

Well, if you don't want to end up as a human ice cream cone, there are other ways to extend your life. Now here's your chance to put them into practice!

CHAPTER EIGHT

IMMORTALITY AT LAST!

So, you've read this book and still think eternal life is just the ticket? Well, unless you're getting on a bit, you don't have to worry about aging just yet. So why not wait twenty years and volunteer for the first-ever life-extension program?

Step One, 2020: Go for a Checkup

All volunteers for the program begin by seeing their doctors for a full checkup. Your doctor makes a CD of your DNA and checks it for any sign of disease or damage.

Step Two, 2020: Still at the Doctor's

Hopefully your DNA is fine, but it might need a course of telomerase treatment to lengthen your telomeres. (These are the protective caps on your chromosomes, remember?) If worse comes to worst, you might need gene implants in some of your organs to ensure that the telomerase gene is switched on for a few years.

Step Three, 2030: The Robot Hospital and Organ Bank

It is time for a routine operation to remove some of your stem cells and freeze them for the future. (The cells can be frozen so fast that they don't suffer ice damage.) After the nanorobots have done their job, you sign autographs and take part in a 3-D holographic TV chat show. (Joining the life-extension program has made you a real celebrity!)

Step Four, 2030: At Home

Back home it's time for a virtual reality chat with Wanda, your personal health adviser. She's been programmed by your doctor to tell you what exercise and diet you need to keep your body in tip-top condition. You'll need to take a complete range of vitamins and antioxidants, but luckily Wanda is not suggesting the dreaded reduced-food diet! By the way, Wanda is a computer-generated being, so she won't age. And she can even teach you computer games to keep your brain in good condition!

Step Five, 2060: Back at the Doctor's

Life has been great so far, and you're still feeling young and fit. But the doctor says your muscles could use some boosting. Luckily, human growth hormone injections are now possible without fear of side effects. You decide to enter the World Senior Citizen Olympics.

Step Six, 2070: Back at the Robot Hospital

You only pop in for a routine checkup, but they offer you the chance to have a complete genetic makeover! All your aging genes are switched off, and the genes that keep you young are replaced.

Despite all the treatment, your kidneys and heart are not what they used to be. And your vision and hearing are weakening. Now it's time to use those stem cells you stored away fifty years ago. In a few months the hospital grows you a new heart and kidneys, and these are transplanted into your body. You opt for the latest bionic eyeballs and ears and leave the hospital with better vision and hearing than you ever had before!

Step Seven, 2120: Back at the Hospital

You're over one hundred years old, but thanks to regular hormone treatment and telomerase fill-ups, you look and feel about thirty. Unfortunately, your lungs and stomach are showing signs of aging, and you're wheezing and suffering from indigestion. But technology has once again come to your rescue. Injections of stem cells can now regenerate your organs without transplants. Phew!

Step Eight, 2130: Back at the Hospital

There's a problem—your old brain is showing signs of aging. The brain contains your personality, so you can't simply plop in someone else's. And because brain cells don't divide, you can't boost them with fast-dividing stem cells. So you opt for the latest artificial bionic brain computer.

All your memories are downloaded into the machine, and it's placed inside your skull. Once the computer is switched on, it's easy to forget that your brain is a machine. Oh well, it should be good for a few hundred years! You celebrate by telling a historian about life back in the 2000s.

Step Nine, 2160: Back at the Robot Hospital

Deep down you feel uneasy. Maybe you've done it all? You've reached level 600 on every interactive virtual reality computer game on the Internet, you've traveled to every country in the world twice, and you're bored with your great, great, great, great, great grandchildren. Fortunately Wanda has the solution—a short cryo-rest. So you arrange to be deep-frozen for a short time, about fifty years.

Step Ten, 2210: That's Better!

You wake up feeling refreshed, if a little chilly. Technology has moved on, and now there's plenty more to do. Scuba diving on Mars is a must now that they've put an ocean there, and skiing on Pluto sounds really cool. You're really looking forward to the next two hundred years. Life is good, and you just can't get enough of it!

CHAPTER NINE

WHO WANTS TO LIVE FOREVER?

Eternal life sounds pretty good, doesn't it? But is immortality everything it's cracked up to be? On the one hand, you have an eternity to do all the things you enjoy. But on the other hand, you've got all the time in the world to get tired of eating your favorite food, watching the same old films and music, and listening to your best friends with their endlessly repeated jokes.

And what about all those old people? You're not going to be the only person living forever. Once they realize how well it's worked, everyone will want the same treatment. The government will have to make sure everyone has a chance to benefit from this technology even if they can't afford it. It would be unfair if the only people who got to live forever were rich, greedy old millionaires. And once there are lots of older people around, how will they be treated?

It is fact, not fantasy, that in the future old people are going to be fitter and healthier, and there are going to be a lot of them. Even without everlasting life treatment, by 2050 in China alone, there will be 270 million people aged over 65. And all these people must be housed and fed and cared for. Perhaps people will stop having children to stop the world from getting overcrowded.

Ultimately, no matter how long life is, it's what you make of it that really counts. Surely seventy good years are better than seven hundred boring ones. So get out there and make the most of however many years you have to live on this planet. And remember— never say die!